HOW TO GROW ORGANIC VEGETABLES IN CONTAINERS (…ANYWHERE!)

How To Grow Organic Vegetables In Containers (...anywhere!)

- what you can grow
- where you can grow
- how you set up
- everything you'll need

Eileen Logan

Writers Club Press
New York Lincoln Shanghai

How To Grow Organic Vegetables In Containers (...anywhere!)

Writers Club Press
an imprint of iUniverse, Inc.

For information address:
iUniverse, Inc.
2021 Pine Lake Road, Suite 100
Lincoln, NE 68512
www.iuniverse.com

The gardening techniques contained herein are well recognized and practiced. These methods have worked in our gardens for years. We hope that you find the same to be true in your gardens. If for some reason they are not, we cannot be held responsible for crop failure, poor harvest or your expenditures. Sometimes nature acts and reacts in certain ways and doesn't consult anyone before it does so.

ISBN: 0-595-21772-9 (Pbk)
ISBN: 0-595-75782-0 (Cloth)

Printed in the United States of America

Preface...

When I thought about writing this book, I was working in my garden, wondering if anyone would actually be interested in this type of planting. After all, one can go to the market and buy vegetables. And, depending upon where you live, there are farm stands selling fresh-picked produce.

But then I got to thinking about the truth.

The truth is that the human body contains many complex sets of components which interact variously. The body has an interdependency unto itself that makes it almost a self-contained unit. Excluding genetic predestiny, the weakest link in the health chain of our body is what we put in it and do to it.

It occurred to me then, that if these factors made for our weaknesses, that is precisely where we should launch an attack to build strength or rebuild health.

Good health begins with our immune system. It is a functionally connected set of glands, membranes, flora, cells, fluids and tissues which include the epidermal, respiratory, digestive, systemic, circulatory, cellular and lymphatic systems.

Our ability to throw off a cold or illness, keep allergies at bay, improve mental acuity, physical stamina or simply enhance the daily quality of life—all originate within our immune system.

If we feed our bodies with vegetables that contain chemicals, our immune system must unite to defend against elements which are foreign. Pesticides, some of which are designed to attack the nervous systems of insects, are an example of a foreign element.

Back to the weak link.

Let's keep it simple. We know that humans have been evolving for centuries without using pesticides or chemical sprays on vegetables. Whether your ancestors grew vegetables in their own gardens or purchased vegetables from others, the type of synthetic chemical sprays we see in today's current use completely did not exist until the early to mid portion of the 1900's.

Incidentally, depending on whomever you believe, neither did a lot of environmental illnesses.

Ah, the price of progress.

Clearly, we are living in a time when our world is changing faster than it ever, ever has before. With these rapid changes, we see an acceptance, a wearied resignation if you will, of ignoring our nutritive health. Why else would market shelves be stocked with an abundant variety of microwavable items and prepackaged, processed, preserved foods?

People may indeed desire to have a selection of fresh, organic vegetables, but feel limited to purchase what is offered commercially; and in return, be willing to surrender up personal choice—something I could never do.

That is when I went full cycle on the truth, and made the commitment to write about how incredibly easy it is to grow vegetables in this manner.

You *can* plant and grow a successful harvest of food for your table. You *can* exercise control over choice and quality. You *can* contribute to your body's good health and support the earth.

You can.

Make it a good day!

Eileen Logan
Los Angeles

To Nana,
who was my first teacher
of all the Earth could offer;
I love you
and
I miss you pal,
I'll see you again come one fine day.

To Jack,
who just loved being outdoors;
boy, did you have the right idea,
we still call you "friend."

To my family, friends and co-workers,
who were so supportive when
I remembered things incorrectly and
forgot them perfectly.

To those incredibly special people,
some of whom
—regrettably—
have come and gone,
but all of whom helped me
to always
stay with my convictions.

And,
to my absolute greatest supporter;
thanks for the faith in me, son,
the feeling is very, very mutual,
I have faith in you and I love you back,
"okay...okay..."

Acknowledgements...

Thanks to the following people who volunteered to give up their lunch—an hour of afternoon sun on a beautiful California day— simply to help me get some of the Glossary alphabetized: B.A.; C.A.; E.M.; I.N.; R.P.; Y.S.; C.S.; J.V.; B.Y. and M.Z. *"Gracias...muchas, muchas gracias. Life is real, guys. Go honestly after the things you want and be the very best at everything you set out to do. This is how you will make it."*

Thanks to **Sam** for the font work on the front cover. I appreciated everything that you actually ever did that actually ever got done. *"Well, if you want my opinion..."*

Thanks to **G'vine** for being such good people and helping me achieve my goals. I could not have done a thing without your help. *"Did you send a statement? Did I get a statement? How much was the statement that you sent that I got?! Oh...Well, when was it due?"*

Thanks to **B.N.** for waving the magic wand and making everything appear to be so easily accomplished. Your forthright business demeanor was what it took to get the job done. *"This is what I need, this is what I want. Now, how do we get there from here...?"*

Thanks to **E.J.** for pinch-hitting. *"I don't have time to explain myself...okay?"*

Thanks to **H.G.** for the input. The depth of my thanks is quality-based and as such, not related to the quantity of words with which I express it. *"Ain't life grand? We live in a country where a person can accomplish anything which they set their mind to...that they possess a capability for...and I'm having a really great time doing precisely that."*

Thanks to **C.L.** for enduring the countless pizzas and deli sandwiches while I kept plugging away. One day, soon I hope, all this will be behind us. *"I love you."*

Thanks to **everyone else** who helped me along the way during the course of this book. I try to give back daily to all that I meet— children, animals, elderly, plants…each thing counts when you're giving back.

*"From the earth,
to the earth."*

Contents

Preface… v

Acknowledgements… ix

1 A Shopping List of Things to get started 1

2 Planting the Seed Pots 9

3 Transplanting Seedlings into Containers 13

4 The very valuable practice of Cultivation 25

5 How to make your own garden compost 29

6 What you really can grow in containers 36

7 Pests 41

8 Tools of the Trade 46

9 Fertilize this! 54

10 Just Maintain 58

11 Harvest Time and Clean–up 61

Appendix I A Glossary of a Certain Sort 65

Appendix II Resources 103

Afterthoughts… 105

About the Author 107

1

"What in the world was I thinking
when I thought I could grow vegetables
out here?"

OR

A Shopping List of Things to get started

Relax. This book is about one of the most wonderful activities you can do to enhance the overall quality of your life. As reports from an ever widening range of researchers, such as health-care specialists to psychologists, life scientists to botanists, continue to document, the benefits of gardening are multitudinous and positive.

First off, it is exercise to the body as one or the other of your limbs is in constant movement. You may have certain medical considerations which preclude lifting, but that is about the only part requiring help from another. Common sense tells us to always take special care with our back and neck. No one will think lesser of you for having an assistant helping you with the set-up.

Working a garden is also a pressure valve for the anxieties of our 21st century life style. When you are working in **your** garden, the beauty of life and science mixes into a creativity that you share. Frankly, no matter what your beliefs about religion or energy force, we can all agree that there is a powerful influence of some type. You are caused into appreciation as you care for your plants. Emotionally and mentally, you are refreshed.

A direct and important benefit to your nutritional health comes from eating vegetables that have **no pesticides, no herbicides, no fungicides, no mildewcides and are not sprayed with preservatives.** You are indeed what you eat and given a choice in the matter, do you want to ingest any of these things? We thought not!

It sounds like you are ready to get started. As follows is a detailed set-up list to check off and follow for organizing your garden. Congratulations, it will be a great success!

1. YOUR DESIRE TO GROW FRESH, ORGANIC VEGETABLES

Ahh, the great outdoors! Although this means different things to each of us, we at least agree that clean, wholesome vegetables to feed ourselves and those we love are part of it. Your interest has motivated you to learn how easily lush, beautiful, organic vegetables can be handily grown just about anywhere. A ground floor balcony, back doorstep or patio can become a productive space for container planting. Following this, simple plant maintenance becomes the actual day-to-day issue.

2. NOTE THE SUN AND SHADE ROTATION OF THE PROPOSED AREA

Would you thrive in a situation adverse to human survival? Neither will a plant which you attempt to grow in improper conditions. The orientation and length of available sunshine will impact what you can grow. Observe the changing conditions of your outdoor area. An area with full sun can grow most summer vegetables. However, any range of sun provides for opportunity and there are many vegetables which cannot tolerate full sun, such as lettuce and most greens.

If you get only indirect sun, but if you get it for most of the day, you will still be able to grow certain crops!

3. PURCHASE ORGANIC, TRADITIONAL OR HEIRLOOM SEEDS/SEEDLINGS

Here is a quick lesson on why you must buy and use these types of seeds and/or seedlings. Organic, traditional and heirloom seeds have been adapting to the environment for generations. They have an inherent genetic resistance to pests and climatic changes. They also have superior nutritional values. One crucial fact to know is that these types of plants will furnish you with seeds that reproduce true to form, year after year. There are enormous varieties of these types of vegetable seeds and seedlings easily available for you to purchase.

A quick footnote, but important to know, is that these seeds grow plants which are open-pollinated. You will want to plan your container locations with this in mind. For example, planting two different varieties of squash from the same squash family in close proximity will likely give you a mixed-cross between the two. Although any seed salesperson worth a grain of compost can provide assistance, you can identify this on your own by reading the formal botanical name of the vegetable.

Be sure and purchase flower seeds or seedlings when planning your container garden. We have used portulaca, aster, zinnia and blue salvia, all of which can be grown in containers. Flowers attract bees which will assist in pollinating your vegetable plants. A good pollination process usually equals a high quality harvest. An added perk to some of these flowers is that they also attract butterflies and hummingbirds.

Please see **Appendix II—Resources** which lists a company from whom you can purchase these types of seeds and seedlings.

4. PURCHASE CLEAN,
RICH UNTAINTED SOIL

Do what?! How? There are several great brands of bagged soil and compost which are 100% organic. Many contain forest and animal by-products making them plenteous with nutrition. Whether buying from the small family-owned nursery or the garden departments of large variety stores, you will be able to find exactly what you need.

5. ASK FOR OLD 6-PACK CONTAINERS
TO USE AS SEED STARTERS

While at your nursery making the above purchase, ask them nicely if you may have a few of their empty 6-pack or 4" containers. You will need these small containers to house germinating seeds and young seedlings. Our experience is that most nurseries will give you a few. Their supply is usually relevant to how many small plants were just transplanted to larger pots, so be gracious…you can always come back for more!

6. BUY A NEW SPRAYER BOTTLE AND REUSE AN OLD WATER BOTTLE

When watering new seeds to bring them to germination, you cannot flush the soil with water as it will disturb the seeds. However, the soil must be kept very moist. We recommend using a new, unused spray bottle for small seeds and a 1 litre size water bottle with a sipper for most all others. You will use these to saturate the soil until residual water comes out the bottom.

7. CONTAINERS

Use the soil spacing guide on the seed packets to help you plan this purchase, or check in the "**What you** *really* **can grow in Containers**" section. There is an ample supply of containers from which to purchase at the garden department of the large variety stores. Do *not* scrimp on this one by purchasing a smaller size. You couldn't live with any measure of health in cramped quarters and neither will your vegetables. Be sure the containers you select have drainage holes in the bottom and are not merely decorative pots.

8. FELT PEN AND POPSICLE STICKS FOR MARKERS

We like popsicle sticks because they are recyclable and hold up to the elements. Although you must use something, it doesn't matter what, as long as you know which little plant popping up is which and when you planted it.

*　　　　　*　　　　　*

There now, doesn't that feel do-able so far? It is! Of the entire eight items, only five must be bought, the other three come from you. The way we see it, the seeds, soil, planters, spray bottle, and marker which you initially buy are either reusable or replenishable, which makes them both an earth-friendly and pocketbook-friendly purchase.

Ready to plant?

Photograph I: Pictured here are two great ways to water a germinating seed bed and seedlings: on the left, a water bottle with sipper; on the right, a water spray bottle with an adjustable nozzle. Both of these give you the control needed for the early stages which a watering can and hose can't give.

Photograph II: Full–growth containers recommended look like this large unit pic-tured and measure 24" tall, 21" in top diameter and 18" in bottom diameter; also use-ful for some crops are five gallon units which measure 12" tall and 10" in diameter; long "tray–type" units that vary in measure from 6"—8" tall, 6"—8" wide and 18"—24" long; or one gallon units which measure 7" tall and 6" in diameter. Remember, it is crucial to understand the soil spacing needs of the variety which you are planting and to use a container appropriate to those needs. We can't stress this enough to you—it is absolutely critical that your plants have an above–adequate space for roots to spread.

2

"Now what am I supposed to do?"

OR

Planting the Seed Pots

Okay, we understand that about now you are so eager and feel like planting all the seeds in every packet. And yes, we accept partial responsibility for this! Let prudence be your guide at this point. Remember, every seed you plant will likely germinate and sprout. That makes you responsible for taking care of a living thing. So, unless you have friends who will gladly accept the gift of a vegetable seedling, we suggest initially planting only two or three seeds of each variety you are planning on container planting. If you are a completely new vegetable gardener, we also suggest starting with hardier seeds which are larger and easier to grow.

A strong consideration here at planting onset is when your days off work and at home are. If, as most of us do, you work Monday through Friday, you will want to start this after work Friday or first thing Saturday morning. Soil will dry out very, very fast in these small containers. Hanging around the house for the weekend will ensure that ample moisture is provided at a very critical time.

We hope you discover joy in what you are about to do. Let us again applaud you for making these choices!

      *   *   *

Begin with the popsicle sticks, small containers, seed packets and soil. Using your hands or a trowel, fill each of the 6-pack sections or 4" containers to the top with soil. Firm the soil down with your fingers. Use a popsicle stick to make a planting hole in the middle of the soil appropriate to the depth instructions for the seed on the packet. Drop the seed in, wish it the best of luck and cover it up with soil. Mark the popsicle stick **immediately** with the name of the plant and stick it in next to the side of the container, away from the planted seed. Plant all your seeds in this manner.

If you have a kitchen calendar or day planner handy, it is a good idea to write down the date you expect germination. Each seed packet normally supplies the projected amount of days for germination, and this is important to make note of.

With respect to how much water is too much or too little, let us advise you to use simple common sense here. Remember, too much water will actually "drown" the seed and not allow the soil to provide a "bed" for the seed. Insufficient amounts of water will not spur the germination process forward and will not release nutrients from the soil which the seed needs for growth.

So what do you do?

Simple! Use your water bottle with sipper for larger seeds and the sprayer bottle for smaller seeds. (A bean seed would be considered a larger seed whereas an onion would be considered a smaller seed.) Go slowly for the first watering after your initial planting, as there will be pockets of air that fill with water and settle the soil. When water starts to seep out the bottom, stop watering. You have saturated the soil and the germination process will has begun.

Feel the moist surface of the soil with your fingertips. How does it feel to you? How would you define it? It will likely remind you of a wet sponge. Consider this "wet sponge" feeling as what you will aim for each time you moisten the soil during the germination process.

*　　　　　*　　　　　*

Your next consideration will be with what frequency to spritz the soil, and this is quite easily determined.

Every hour or so after planting, use the fingertip method and touch the soil. Slight drying out is normal and good because this is when the seed is absorbing nutrients and moisture from the soil. The trick is to not let it dry out too much and stop the germination process.

So! Our advice here is to become one with the seed. Really! "Become the seed." Use your fingertips to tell your brain what the moisture level of the soil is. When in doubt on moist versus dry, it is better to error on an extra spritz.

Before going to bed, you should heavy-spritz again as you first did at original planting. Upon awakening, do the same thing again. Give everything a good, healthy spritz to greet the day. Continue to follow through over the weekend in this manner. When Monday comes, water as soon as you get up. When you are ready to leave for work, give one "good" watering for the day.

Until your seeds germinate, it would be a great idea to come straight home from work and water them. In a sense, it's almost like having a child or a pet!

*　　　　　*　　　　　*

"A watched pot never boils." Any cook will tell you this is a true statement and scientific evidence *certainly* supports it. After you have planted the seeds, diligently watered the soil, checked thirty seven times a day for any progress and have seen precisely NOTHING…you may start to wonder if something has gone wrong. It is at this time when you should remember the old wives tale and apply it to your gardening.

Waiting for your seeds to sprout is a great time to cherish and admire nature. You will start to appreciate how unique and marvelous nature is. How does the seed know what to do? What is it doing in the dark soil? Trust nature to know when it is the right time for the seed to sprout and trust yourself. You have done your part correctly.

*   *   *

In our gardens, where the wind has blown and redistributed seeds from a previous planting, a verde tomatillo may pop up in a garlic pot, or a parsnip continues to thrive and sprout new seed umbrels season after season. Others have said it before and we agree.

Nature is a heckuva thing.

Before you know it, a little sprout of green will pop up through the soil. You will cheer, give toast to life and be another step on your way to fresh vegetables.

Let us take a moment to congratulate you on your success. We understand how special this simple moment is and we are happy for you! Enjoy the feeling and tuck it into your heart to save.

3

"So, where are the vegetables?"

OR

Transplanting Seedlings into Containers

This is a wonderful time to be in the garden. Each plant is full of hope and the promise of nutrition. You may find this interval harder to endure than waiting for the seeds to germinate!

When your seedlings have six to eight true leaves, it is time to transplant them into their permanent home. Although you must understand the basic fundamentals of how to do the actual transplanting—we want you to know that, unless you are rough or negligent in your handling of a seedling, there simply isn't much you can do to damage a plant at this point. So, relax.

Follow these guidelines, but follow your senses. Is your touch too hard? Too soft? What does the soil feel like? Since these are living things, you will want to pay close attention to them. When you transplant your seedlings, take a moment to examine the wonder of their root system. Kiss the leaves! We have!

Do pay attention to the instructions regarding how close together you may plant the seedlings and trust this sage advice. For the large containers we recommend using, two bush bean plants will fit nicely. Yet, the same container will only fit a single squash plant.

Yes, yes—we know, it is only a tiny little plant. How big could it get? Well, consider an answer in these terms: How big were you when you were born? We rest our case!

*   *   *

We have included two sources of step-by-step directions for the transplantation of your seedlings within the following pages. People learn differently and in different ways. Some people do well with reading directions, and some people need to see pictures. We offer both!

Photograph III: A broccoli seedling in a 4" seedling starter pot ready for transplant to a container. Be sure to water your seedlings first and get the soil soaked. That way, the entire root system will slide out much easier and with less disturbance. A seedling can go into shock if the fragile root system is displaced.

Photograph IV: With one hand supporting the bottom surface of the seedling starter pot, put the other hand over the top surface, spreading your fingers open and resting on the soil with the stalk between your index and middle fingers. Think of your hands in two ways, a "plant" hand and a "pot" hand. Nothing need be grabbed or pulled, gravity will do all the work once it is turned over.

Photograph V: Until you get the hang of it, we advise standing near the final container that the seedling is being transplanted into. You may even want to do this step directly above the container, just in case things happen faster than you thought! With your "plant" hand still in place, use your "pot" hand to rotate the seedling starter pot over; some loose soil may fall out, but the seedling, the root system and the supportive soil (seedling unit) will be safely embraced within your "plant" hand and the seedling starter pot.

Photograph VI: This is an all-at-once action that can sometimes happen very quickly. First, grasp the seedling starter pot with your "pot" hand and slowly pull it up. As you do, the seedling unit should start to slide out underneath. Use your entire "plant" hand to balance the seedling unit and just let the seedling starter pot fall where you stand.

Photograph VII: While keeping your "plant" hand in the original position, support the newly posed soil/root area of the seedling unit with your [now] free hand; that is to say, with the hand at was the "pot" hand. Rotate the seedling unit upright.

Photograph VIII: Continue to lightly hold the seedling on the top and bottom, as previously. U both hands for full support and begin to rotate the seedling unit towards the prepared hole in t container.

Photograph IX: It is very important that you do not allow the seedling unit to drop into the container at this point. Doing so could create air space next to the roots, which when back-filled can actually cause a root disturbance and send your beautiful seedling into shock. Instead, gently rotate the seedling unit into the prepared hole.

Photograph X: Backfill with container soil, adding more from your soil bag if need be. Use *your* *whole hand to firmly pat down the soil and make a plant bed. The soil surface under your seed* *should be slightly lower that the soil surface of the container, to capture water and direct it down to* *root system. Next, gently water only the 6"–8" area around the stalk.*

Doesn't this look incredibly easy? It really is. However, we suggest that you read the following additional directions and information before you begin. That way you can be completely confident about what you are doing! Position the container where you intend to grow the plant, because a container full of soil is a very hard thing to move.

- ➢ Fill the container with soil to within three or so inches of the top. If this is a "full sun" vegetable, you may find that mulch will help keep the soil from drying out. If you are adding mulch, pour a one inch layer of mulch on top. Loosely mix the mulch and the soil together.
- ➢ In the middle of the container use your hand trowel to make a planting hole approximately the same size as your transplant pot. (Remember the six-packs and small starter pots?) If you are transplanting two seedlings, make two holes equal distance from each other and the side of the planter. If your seedlings are in six-packs, carefully cut the segments apart at the top with scissors first.
- ➢ Since the seedling and its root system will come out much easier if they are moist, take just a moment to water them.
- ➢ Now, holding the bottom of the transplant pot with one hand, place the other hand over the top of the seedling so that the stem and leaves poke through between your index and middle finger. No need to grab the leaves or apply any pressure. If you do, you may break the stem and in doing so, kill the seedling.
- ➢ Turn the transplant pot over and **gently** shake it up and down until the seedling slides out. Let the small pot drop. Keep the soil around the root system intact as much as possible during the short transport time to the container. A major disturbance to the root system at this step can cause a plant to stunt its growth, or worse, to die.
- ➢ Keep the seedling and the soil encasing the roots cupped in your hand. At the container carefully "right" the seedling, by using both

hands to rotate the root system into the planting hole which you have previously made.

➢ Once the seedling is in the planting hole, carefully backfill empty spots with soil. After you have done that, press all of the surface soil in the container down firmly, just as if you are tucking the plant in to bed!

➢ You will need to use your water bottle at this point to give the transplant a good watering. However, there is no reason to water so heavily that the water seeps out the bottom of the container. All that is necessary now is that the root area gets sufficiently watered. To that extent, water in a 6" – 8" inch diameter around the stem of the transplant until the soil feels soggy.

          *   *   *

Then…admire yourself. Look at the wonderful task which you have successfully completed. Take pictures! Our first year of crops was a photo opportunity of excessiveness if there ever was!

4

"What do you mean,
help my plants to breathe?"

OR

The very valuable practice of Cultivation

We are constantly asked about shortcutting this action, to which a sustained "boo-hiss" has become the standard reply!

Consider this scenario:

As a rule, you brush your teeth in the morning and again at night. Whether in the morning or evening, you shower or bathe daily. During your bath or shower, you always wash your hair, your face and your body.

Then one day, you don't.

The next day, you don't do anything either.

Day after day, you do none of the above. In fact, you actually decide that this is how life is going to be for you. After all, isn't it a lot easier to bypass these rituals? Just think of all the extra time you'll have to do other things!

How realistic would this be for you? Can you make the analogy to living things like your vegetable plants? Well, of course you can. This is why you are as wonderful as you are.

*   *   *

Cultivation is "roughing up" the top layer of soil around your plants with a tool called a cultivator. A hand cultivator is a small, multi-pronged tool. In the early days of our garden, *anything* was being used as a cultivating tool! Screwdrivers, small pots...there is some slight memory of even using a pen!

When you cultivate your plants, you furnish them with an aerated soil which allows water to drain evenly into the container, be absorbed by the soil and metabolized by the roots. Cultivation also disturbs any weed growth or adverse bacterial growth within the soil—which will preclude your plant from being detrimentally affected by them.

Another very important function of cultivation is that it keeps the soil from compacting. In severe cases of soil compaction, water almost completely bypasses roots and simply drains out the bottom.

Photograph XI: Cultivators are a really important tool to have and regularly use. We can't think
ny permanent, acceptable stand-in for them. When you buy yours, look for one that has a com-
able grip. Cultivating is a repetitive motion and your wrist will tire easily if you have an uncom-
able handle.

Regular cultivation should be done every one or two weeks for each plant. Don't cultivate deeper than the depth of the cultivator's prongs or you will start to get into your plants root territory. Don't get closer to the stalk than 3"–4" or you may disturb the root ball of the plant and cause it to weaken or lodge over.

Every four weeks it is a great idea to mix in compost or fertilizer when cultivating. By doing so, nutrients get dispersed within the soil, allowing for their easy assimilation by the root system whenever you water. When the temperature starts to get warmer and the soil seems to dry out faster than you can water, you may need to mulch your plants. Doing so will help them to retain water within the soil and channel a steady supply of moisture to the growing vegetables. Use the hand cultivator to mix in the mulch. We have found that the moisture-holding properties of mulch respond much better and benefit plants more when they are cultivated into the soil, versus a topical application.

The point here is that cultivation is a completely necessary action which you must undertake on behalf of all the plants in your garden. Vegetables, flowers or herbs—be they growing in surface soil or in containers…are all parts of a living ecosystem which you have formed.

Treat them right!

5

"You want me to do what?"

OR

How to make your own garden compost

Composting is one of the more important and fundamental parts of organic home gardening. It is a methodology involving aeration, heat and moisture; wherein organic matter is blended into a soil mixture and allowed to decompose within the confinement of a composter or similar containment. The decomposing organic matter, over time, turns into "humus." This rich, vital, organic humus now contains the plenteous nutrients from the decomposed matter.

You can make your own compost anywhere from a small apartment or condominium scale, all the way to a grand piece of land scale. What you choose will depend on the available outdoor space you have, your gardening needs and how much you want to spend on a composter. However, if your residence does not lend itself to composting, it is possible to buy ready-made compost. If you want to make your own, our advice for the first season is to start on a small scale.

The amount of space available is the primary determinant for what method of composting will work best for you, because it is the most functional aspect. If you are working with extremely limited space, you will only be able to make small batches. The opposite is likewise true, if you have a huge back patio slab, you can make a huge pile of compost.

A second factor is how much money you desire to spend on making or purchasing a composter. There are certainly a lot of composters available for sale, and most of them deliver as promised. However, please know that some composters merely contain great advertising and nothing else.

Let us remind you of the famous quote from P.T. Barnum, para-phrased and rewritten thusly, "There is a foolish gardener born every minute."

The very best backyard composter we have ever found for small gardens is called a "Spinning Composter" and is available through a supplier found in the "**Resources**" appendix in the back of this book. We also like this composter because it doesn't require you to aerate the soil. Just turn it and the composter does the aeration for you.

Photograph XII: Our own wonderful spinning composter, currently full of decomposing goodies. This unit stands 26" tall and 18" wide.

Now, what goes in your composter?

Let this motto be your guide: "From the Earth, to the Earth." For example, you can compost the balance of uneaten carrots from dinner, but not if they were buttered. Butter is a processed food, a by-product, and as such not "From the Earth." We would likely rinse the butter off with hot water and then throw the carrots into the composter.

Any leftover meats, which although coming directly from an animal, have been processed by virtue of cooking. These cannot be composted as they will turn rancid and are unable to decompose in the sense of the word used here. Any dairy product, such as cheeses or eggs, should not be composted for the same reason. However, you can compost egg shells.

Whew! Ready for a quick and easy list of "around the house" stuff that you *can* compost? Okay, here it is!

✓ bark
✓ bread [*stale*]
✓ cat fur [*as long as animal is healthy*]
✓ cereal [*past usage dates*]
✓ coffee grains
✓ corn cobs [*they will take a loooong time*]
✓ 100% cotton ear swabs [*used, yes - used*]
✓ dog fur [*as long as animal is healthy*]
✓ feathers [*again from a healthy bird*]
✓ fruit, fruit cores and skins/peels
✓ grass clippings [*avoid if exposed to chemical treatments; dog or cat urine or feces*]
✓ hay [*new or used*]

✓ **human hair** [*as long as person is healthy & hair isn't chemically treated*]

✓ **leaves**

✓ **lint** [*as long as it is from natural fibers, like cotton or linen*]

✓ **manure** [*chicken, rabbit, horse, cow*]

✓ **mushrooms**

✓ **newspapers**

✓ **packing "peanuts"**

✓ **peanut shells**

✓ **plant debris** [*as long as plants are healthy and without pests*]

✓ **potatoes**

✓ **sawdust**

✓ **seaweed**

✓ **tea bags**

✓ **vacuum cleaner catches** [*empty bag directly into composter*]

✓ **vegetables** [*old/unused as well as trimmings and table scraps*]

✓ **weeds** [*without weed seeds*]

✓ **wood ashes**

This list is a well-rounded compilation of standard household fare that should get you underway. However, if you are a single person and just don't generate that much waste or do not have access to many things on the list, you may have to find some outside resources for organic material. Your community may have a program which allows you to pick up usable items for composting. Also, your local market may regularly throw out their vegetable trimmings and not mind it a bit if you picked them up instead. As with anything else, the more you look, the more you find.

Once you have gotten your compost started, you will want to mix in some activators. An activator is something that is high in nitrogen and will aid your compost in the decomposition process. Used in proper proportions, activators can actually start to generate heat within the compost pile. It is this heat, as well as moisture and aeration, that over time aids the decomposition of the organic matter into rich humus.

Some activators which are easy to find and inexpensive to purchase include: bat guano; chicken manure; cottonseed meal; blood meal and grass clippings. We recommend starting each new batch of compost with a base of ready-made humus. If your compost already includes nitrogen-rich things (grass clippings, chicken manure and so forth)—it is less likely to need a high dose of an activator.

The best time to start a new compost pile is in the spring, because the days are starting to warm up. If you try to compost in cooler or cold weather, you may have a very unsatisfactory time of it.

Put your composter in the full sun and where there is an accommodation for water run-off. You will have to wet the compost in the beginning and from time to time to aid in the decomposition.

In theory, you should turn your compost every week or two to aerate it. We generally turn ours every couple of days and then not again for a week or two. Then, we rotate it every few days and again in a week or two. It's a pattern. We found ours, you will find yours.

Remember, you are going to be continually adding wastes and trimmings to your composter. When the finished product is ready and available to use on plants, it will look like a dark, rich soil and have a very earthy smell. Use your hand trowel to scoop out the humus, throwing back anything not yet decomposed.

Garden compost is a compilation of the richest nutrients that a plant can receive. Every three to four weeks, liberally apply a handful or two of compost to your plants and mix it in with your cultivator. By mixing it with the surface soil of a plant, the nutrients are channeled to the roots every time you water.

You can also make a compost tea for a quick plant "pick-me-up" by soaking compost in water overnight and draining the water into a sprayer. Use the compost tea directly from the sprayer on the plant leaves. You may also find that your seedlings, which don't yet have a highly developed root system, will reap a nutritional benefit if you switch every so often from a "regular" watering to a "compost tea" watering.

When provided with regular compost applications, your garden plants will be bursting with health and also be better able to successfully defend against pest infestation. It's such a positive cycle: *you* are helping take care of your vegetable plant's health and your vegetable plants will help take care of *your* health!

6

"My eyes are bigger than my stomach!"

OR

What you really can grow in containers

There are a lot more vegetables which you *can* grow in containers than vegetables which you *cannot*.

Every one of these plants listed below has been grown in our gardens. We hope you find many of your favorites. If you don't, look to see if something comparable in vegetable harvest size and plant spacing needs is shown. If so, you can feel entirely confident in growing your favorites!

For purposes of providing you with a spacial perspective, all plant sizing is referenced to the large container planter [24" x 21" x 18"] shown in **Section 1**. If the plant can be grown in a smaller pot or in trays, it will be noted. If you are not sure, error on the side of *more* container space, *not less*. Just about all annual flowers will do very well in a large to mid-size container.

☐   *amaranth:*
any variety that does not exceed 3—4 feet in height; 1 plant to a large container; if in a windy area, may need eventual staking

☐ *amaranth salad greens:*
2—3 plants to a large container; 1 plant to a 5 gallon container; keep trimming to encourage new growth and slow bolting

☐ *basil:*
2—3 plants to a large container; 1 plant to a 5 gallon container

☐ *beans (fava, pole, bush):*
1—2 plants to a large container; pole beans may need cage or staking depending on variety

☐ *beets:*
2—3 plants to a large container; beets need space for both root and greens growth

☐ *broccoli:*
1 plant to a large container; cutting main head when ready allows for side shoots to fill out and produce nicely

☐ *carrots:*
6—8 standard plants to a large container; if a miniature variety, can grow same quantity in a 5 gallon container

☐ *celery:*
2—3 plants to a large container; 1 plant to a 5 gallon container

☐ *cilantro:*
2—3 plants to a large container; 1 plant to a 5 gallon container; let one cilantro plant go to seed, the seeds are coriander [spice]

☐ *cherry tomatoes:*
1 plant to a large container; may need cage or staking unless a bush variety

☐ *chilies:*
1 plant to a large container; be careful when handling mature plants, the capsicum [hot property] of the chile is present in all parts of the plant, you may forget, rub your eyes after cutting a chile off and give yourself a horrible burn

☐ *chives:*
6—8 plants to a large container; 3—4 plants to a 5 gallon container

☐ *cucumbers (bush and vine):*
1 plant to a large container; vine varieties will need a cage or staking

☐ *dill:*
3—5 plants to a large container; grown for two types of harvest and cooking usage— fresh or dried green leaves and dill seed

☐ *eggplant:*
1 plant to a large container; may require staking for support

☐ *garlic:*
4 bulbs to a large container (evenly spaced); we don't suggest using 1 bulb to a 5 gallon container, we tried and it didn't work; try flavoring your garlic during growth by placing a dried chile pod an inch or two under the soil where you place your bulb, you will harvest spicy garlic when the chile leaches into the soil and is absorbed by the garlic's roots; the opposite is also true, if you have a plant which you would like to enhance with a slight garlic flavor, leave extra room in the container for planting one garlic bulb, [example: cucumbers would be an ideal choice

for this growing trick if you are growing them in order to make refrigerator pickles] "We love garlic."

☐   *kale:*
2—3 plants to a large container

☐   *leeks:*
3—4 plants to a large container

☐   *lettuce:*
2—3 plants to a large container

☐   *mustard greens:*
3—4 plants to a large container

☐   *onions (both green and bulb):*
green—use row planters; bulb—4 to a large container

☐   *parsley:*
2—3 plants to a large container

☐   *parsnips:*
4 plants to a large container

☐   *peas:* (bush or vine); any variety, may need cage or staking; 1 plant to a large container

☐   *peppers:* (sweet, hot and anything in between); any variety; 1 plant to a large container

☐   *radish:* use row planters and space 2"—3" apart

☐   *squash:* (summer varieties—yellow crookneck, scallop, zucchini; although there are *plenty* more) 1 plant to a large container; may need cage or trellis

☐   *sunflowers:* smallish flower heads 12" or less in diameter; 1 plant to a large container

☐   *swiss chard:* any variety; 2—3 plants to a large container

☐   *tomatoes:* (full size); any variety; 1 plant to a large container; may need cage or staking unless a bush variety

☐   *tomatillos:* any variety; 1 plant to a large container

☐   *turnips:* any variety; 2—3 to a large container

*   *   *

That's a bunch of great vegetables! We would find it very difficult to narrow it down to just a few. Good luck!

7

"There are big/small,
green/brown, furry/slimy,
hopping/flying/crawling things
in my garden!"

OR

Pests

The first thing you need to know is that your plants are going to get them. They may not be many in number, however your plants are going to get them.

But, we are getting way, way ahead of ourselves. Let's focus on where you are now.

First in sequential order here, is the simple fact that your container garden is an ecosystem within the environment in which you live.

Now, within both the ecosystem that you've created and the environment in which you live, many organisms also live. The most visible and high profile thing to you in your container garden are your seedlings, which grow to become your plants. Remember though, the soil in the container also houses organisms.

There are good and beneficial organisms, just as there are good and beneficial insects. Likewise, damaging organisms can exist in soil and damaging insects can exist on plants. Since you are container planting, you will be buying fresh soil and shouldn't have to experience damaging soil organisms. It's those pesky insects that are the "pests" of which we speak, and they are as diverse as the varieties of plants upon which they feed.

Each plant can draw their own set of potential pests. A healthy plant is *dramatically* less likely to succumb to pest infestation versus a plant that is lacking in nutrients. Logically then, the initial response of a proactive "pest defense" is to regularly cultivate and fertilize your plants.

Remember, you are growing food for your table. The plants in your garden should be healthy and full of nutrients for you, the end user.

But let's just say that you found *something*, and although you're not quite sure what it is, you definitely know that it isn't a beneficial insect like a lace wing or a lady bug or a praying mantis. What should you do?

For starters, do *not* buy or apply any synthetic or chemical pesticide of *any* nature at all. Remember? Organic? Helloooo? Do not panic and do not quit taking care of your plant.

There's a couple of different ways to go. One way is to acknowledge that harmful insects prey upon sickly plants more often and more severely than healthy plants. Examine the overall health of the plant. Can you make a compost tea for the plant instead of regular water for a week or two? Can you spray compost tea on the leaves? Try to douse the insects while you're at it, as they will hate the taste of the tea.

Truly, this *is* an important point to store in your gardening memory: Spraying compost tea directly on harmful insects, coupled with the subsequent absorption of the tea through the plant's leaves, stalk and roots, will send them a strong message that your plant is not a good choice for a home.

Another way is to try and pick the insects off your plant. If they are worms, there aren't going to be too many that do your plants any favors. Get rid of them. Look for their eggs under your plant's leaves and in the crevices where the leaves shoot out from the stalk.

If your pests are winged insects, try to catch them. If a section of your plant looks severely damaged, you may want to cut it off and remove the trimmings from your garden altogether. Beware though, a fresh cut stalk can invite these little rascals right into your plant. We hope that you mitigate any pest problem before it gets that dramatic.

An alternative thought to include here is that insects provide food for birds. Can you draw birds to the area by placing bread or birdseed? Believe me, birds know where to locate even the smallest aphids—if you invite them into your container garden, they will find the insects.

Photograph XIII: An example of a classic pest. This variety is best known for their abilities to dig up any seedling or plant and relocate it elsewhere, usually to the ground or like area, where it then dries out and becomes useless in the current form, but can provide secondary usefulness in the composter.

Other avenues include earth-friendly soap sprays and garlic sprays, directly applied via a water spray bottle to the affected area or to the insects. These methods certainly stay within organics. Once or twice we have used them on our vegetable crops and flowers.

Unfortunately, these sprays aren't a permanent solution and tend to drip off when the sprinklers come on, in addition to discouraging beneficial insects and birds from stopping by. We'd rather fix the problem than the symptom.

The bottom line here actually takes us back to the beginning. Your garden is an ecosystem within an environment, where things like pests exist.

Pests are opportunistic and will thrive in any place where the factors are right. Eliminate unhealthy conditions in your garden and you will have greatly mitigated your exposure to a pest infestation.

If you do get pests, immediately begin damage control to get them out of your containers. In doing so, try to understand that nature is really about a balance, as it has been for eons. Plants will survive and produce food, people will eat.

Your vegetable plant may not really need your helping hand as much as *you* might need to simply, but deeply, observe nature's balance.

8

"I'll take this and this and this and this and while I'm at it, I'll take this TOO!"

OR

Tools of the Trade

There are shelves and shelves full of items which advertise that they will make your life easier when gardening. Some of them do, some of them don't. Of the ones that do, not all of them are complete necessities.

Stop and think about early civilizations. Did they have corner nurseries? Of course not! Even those brave souls who came to the "New World" had only rudimentary tools, at best, by any standard in use today. So, where do you draw the line between absolute necessity and disposable income spending?

In addition to tools or items shown elsewhere in the book, we feel equipment featured within this section to be further necessities, and will let you take it from there.

When considering a gardening tool purchase, there are a few things which you should think about.

Always buy the best quality which you can honestly afford. Going for the cheapest-priced tools gets you exactly what you paid for over the long run. Definitely shop around for the best prices at your local retailers. Prices vary by as much as 100% from place to place for comparable items.

Admittedly, some tools can double-up and do the work of others. However, each tool has been made for a specific purpose and completes that purpose better than another tool—made for a different purpose—can possibly do. Using the proper tool for the job can mean less frustration for you. Oh sure, we admit to doubling-up on tool usage once upon a time. But, you can bet that as soon as our gardens started to grow and yield prolific harvests, the first things on the list were proper tools!

Have either a storage place or a method of cover up ready for your tools where they won't be exposed to the elements. Yes, they're sturdy and built tough, but continued exposure to the sun and moisture will age tools prematurely and turn them into junk.

There is no set priority list on tools. Some plant varieties which you want to grow will require certain tools, and there will be no getting around it. Your plants will make it just fine if they have to wait a week or two while you shop the stores and get what you really want.

With all this in mind, as follows are our recommendations for gardening necessities.

Photographs XIV and XV: If you plan on working outside in the sun, you must protect your fa neck and hair from the damage which ultraviolet rays can cause. Invest in a pair of cloth gloves [le or vinyl/water repellent gloves [right]. They are a must and will protect your cuticles and skin fr scrapes and planter soil, the latter of which can actually act as an abrasive to your skin.

Photograph XVI: Hand trowels like these come in different sizes depending upon intended usage. The one shown on left may be handy for small scoops of soil, digging holes and backfilling soil; the one on the right for transplanting seedlings or planting any bulbs (including garlic).

Photograph XVII: Weeders are great for pulling out the unwanted visitors that come along from time to time. We have found that weeders can also be useful for locating and digging out root crops like garlic, carrots, beets and so forth, which trowels [and the people using them] often accidentally gouge into.

Photograph XVIII: A cage or circle trellis is mandatory for vining plants, and a "maybe" for any variety that is not classified as a "bush" variety. We also recommend it for any container plant if you are in a high wind area where crops could get blown over and break their stalks.

Photograph XIX: Featured in amongst the beautiful hedge sculptures are soil spades. Shown on the left, a rounded edge spade, used for digging into soil; on the right, a flat edge spade, used for moving a pile of soil from one place to the other. These beat the heck out of lifting a bag or container of soil and straining your back!

Photograph XX: Nippers and clippers—you'll need at least the smaller set to trim and cut most vegetables; the larger may come in useful depending on what you grow.

9

"Eeee–yeee–uuuck"

OR

Fertilize this!

Do you take vitamins or supplements? Do you avoid sodas and junk foods? Do you *try* to eat right? If the answers to these questions are mostly affirmative, then you have a basis from which to understand why your plants need extra nutrients—because it is about that simple.

The packaged soil which you are using is clean soil, without chemicals and additives. Although it may be nutrient rich, it is not a wholly sufficient nutritive environment. Additionally, you lose valuable soil components everytime you water due to above–ground drainage. These two reasons are primarily why you must either make or purchase fertilizer.

A homemade fertilizer (such as compost) is great general purpose nutrition for crops. However, compost takes time to make and will not be ready for use if you are starting it at the same time as seedlings.

Some garden retailers offer wonderful fertilizer choices that are well within the perimeters of the organic market. Remember— even your fertilizer should remain organic! Don't let a nursery owner or gardening department employee tell you that they've never seen such a product. Such an admission is tantamount to an admission of ignorance from them on issues surrounding organic gardening. Organic fertilizer *is* a retail product option available for consumer purchase. All you have to do is find who sells it in your area or a retailer who can order it for you.

Stay committed—even when the person behind the counter tries to tell you that it isn't popular and nobody wants it.

Simply smile and say, "Well, I do…"

*   *   *

A standard recommendation is to fertilize mid to long growth crops every three to four weeks once they have left the seedling stage and are growing toward young plant stage. Short growth plants are exceptions to this rule. As follows are thumbnail guides to know when to fertilize each.

SHORT GROWTH PLANTS

Some food plants have a short growth span of only 30—60 days from germination to flowering to fruiting; or if greens, from germination until you can harvest the first edible leaves. For these, you will need to make some adjustments to ensure that the plants receive proper fertilization.

A helpful pacing method is to work backward from the maturation date listed.

For example, let's say that you have a kale seedling and the seed packet states that young greens can be harvested in as early as 30 days. Calculate the point at which the plant was 50% past seedling stage and into young plant stage.

This is easier to do than it sounds.

If you are seeing leaves that look like each other, come from a very small center growth and progress in size as they grow outwards, then you are seeing edible leaves from a plant emergent in a young plant stage. If it is a 30 day plant, then the point at which you have seen those types of leaves for approximately 15 days is a good time to start fertilizing.

Following this, a small amount of fertilizer every 10 to 14 days will keep your crops healthy and productive.

MID TO LONG GROWTH PLANTS

These types of plants are generally going to be either fruiting plants or root crops and will have a longer growth rate to allow for maturation of the vegetable. Depending on how many containers you have, you may wish to fertilize every plant at the same time, or set up a rotating schedule. Whatever you decide, plan on applying fertilizer every three to four weeks for each plant.

*   *   *

Each type of fertilizer has a different combination of nutrients and purpose. The following are the basic essentials which you may feel confident using in your garden.

- ☞ **cottonseed meal**—*for shade and acid loving plants*
- ☞ **blood meal**—*high in nitrogen for lush green growth and fruiting*
- ☞ **bone meal**—*high in nitrogen, phosphorus and potassium*
- ☞ **fish emulsion**—*high in minerals*
- ☞ **gypsum**—*promotes water absorption and breaks up clay soils*
- ☞ **phosphorus**—*strengthens stems and roots*
- ☞ **hydrated lime**—*assists soil in absorbing fertilizer*

*   *   *

As a general rule, don't fertilize your crops within five days of picking your harvest vegetables. Your plants must assimilate the nutrients from the fertilizer via the soil, and this is not an immediate action. Your vegetables may have a most unpleasant taste if you slip up and forget this!

Familiarize yourself with what type of fertilizer each of your vegetable plants needs. Normally, each seed distributor will print a brief snippet on the back of each packet advising what type of soil mix or fertilizer is best for each plant.

Learn how to quantify the proper amount of fertilizer which your plants need by examining the label recommendations versus plant size. Remember, some of your fertilizer will be draining out the bottom of your container every time you water, so you may want to error by being a tad over rather than less when it comes to actual application.

Remember, not only is fertilizing an integral part of a good pest defense for your garden, it also gives your plants the nutritive building blocks with which they will thrive and flourish you with harvest— and in doing so, enhance the quality of *your* life.

10

"What is going on?
Why is this happening?
What should I do?
What is going on?"

OR

Just Maintain

The interim growth period of vegetable plants is one of the easiest legs of the home gardening journey. The seedling stems have strengthened into hardy stalks. Small flowering buds have pollinated into what is now maturing fruit. Bush plants are bushy and vine plants are vining. What kinds of things could you possibly have to trouble yourself with when everything seems so right?

Not much…but there are a few things which should be underscored.

Follow the printed instructions on your seed packet for proper **crop spacing, sun rotation** and **watering** needs.

Remember to **mulch** your plants if it gets too hot. Although summer plants have the genetic programming to endure summer heat, *a container plant will dry out* and feel heat much more than it would if it were planted in sub grade soil. Keep mulch a few inches away from the main stalk or it will cause the stalk to retain moisture and become diseased.

Cultivate your plants as part of their *regular plant hygiene.* If you're still not a believer, go a day or two without brushing your teeth, combing your hair or washing your face to see how you would feel.

Regularly **fertilize** your vegetable plants so they may enjoy *good nutritive health.*

Keep an eye out for any adverse conditions like **pests** and treat your plants **organically** with **soap sprays, garlic sprays** or picking insects off by hand. Remember, a healthy plant is much, much less likely to succumb to an infestation.

Calendar a growth chart for your plants so that you can be kitchen–ready at **harvest** time.

The best is yet to come!

Photograph XXI: One of our flowering fava bean plants with emergent beans. Yummmie!

11

"Am I supposed to sweep all this under my rug? Or what?"

OR

Harvest Time and Clean–up

Just in case you are wondering if all this hard work you have put in has been worth it, will ever be worth it or has any value whatsoever— let me tell you a story that dates back to our very first organic harvest, some nine years ago.

One of the earliest plants to come in was a salad cucumber. My son was with me in the garden, on what was a very hot Sunday afternoon, when we discovered three or four little beauties ready for picking. As we rinsed the "outdoorsy stuff" off the cukes, we decided to eat them where we stood. The crisp smell from the freshly cut vine was just *so* beckoning.

Crunch. Crunch. Crunch. *Crunch, crunch, crunch.* Next one. Then another. We ate all four cucumbers, right there in the garden next to the plant from which they came. He and I both decided that those cucumbers were the very best treats we had *ever* experienced in vegetables. We agreed that their taste and texture were much better than anything we could have conjured up. They were simply so flavorful.

Although that moment was enough to justify a continuation of home–grown organics, it wasn't until Monday morning arrived that it was cemented it in as a truly permanent lifestyle choice.

Within the first hour of work, at least three co-workers asked me what I had done over the weekend. One noted that it looked like I had gotten a tan. Another said I looked like I had gotten a facial. One gal even went so far as to suggest I had taken a "get–away" weekend from the husband and kids.

"Nope," I said, "I think it's because of cucumbers."

They thought I meant some type of facial mask! When I clarified that I had meant eating a big portion of our super–fantastic, home–grown, organic cukes— they were astonished.

But…think about it. Good, healthy plant soil is rich in many nutrients, like minerals, that are good for humans too. A fresh–cut vegetable which you eat has had literally no time to begin a decomposition process. Therefore, when you eat vegetables—right out of your garden—you are ingesting into your body the maximum amount of minerals that the vegetable has within it and you are doing so within the form most easily assimilated by humans; that being namely…food.

What greater beauty is there to be found than that of vitality in the eyes of a person who enjoys good health?

So…please believe that your hard work is about to come back to you in ways which may be immeasurable in conventional form, or may be as evident as that Monday morning of mine so many years ago.

*   *   *

The seed packet will specify the length of time until harvest or maturity, but it is only a guide. Your plants may have delivered faster or slower than what the seed company stated due to any number of factors. Although you have grown these plants for a table harvest, consider letting one or two of them "go to seed." You may want to grow the same variety again sometime and a plant will biodiversify to the environment in which it lives and reproduces. This fact allows a species to work with the factors in an area and adapt to them, creating a healthy and highly productive strain for your usage.

With respect to a table harvest—and practically speaking, you can look at the vegetable plant and see if either the red tomatoes or yellow squash are still green, or if they are starting to look a bit closer to a ripe vegetable. If you truly can't tell, stick to the harvest guide on the packet. Pick the largest and earliest one you remember seeing…how does it taste? One great thing about growing your own garden is that you have the luxury of time and choice as to when to harvest. Sure, it is perfectly understandable that a potential for some uncertainty exists, but if it looks like a ripe vegetable…smells like a ripe vegetable…it's going to taste like a ripe vegetable.

If your harvest is coming in faster than you can eat or share, most fresh–picked organic vegetables will stay fresh in the refrigerator for a few weeks. Store them just as you picked them, without rinsing. Rinsing will cause them to become slimy and could prompt them into forming a mold. Simply pick the vegetables and wrap them up in a paper or vegetable bag.

Some vegetables can be par–cooked and frozen. Green beans and peas seem to do well this way. Other vegetables can be cooked up in a secondary recipe and frozen. Zucchini bread is a favorite of ours. Vegetable soup is another. It is really a neat feeling to serve up a warm bowl of your own vegetable soup in the middle of a cold winter night.

We wish you good eating!

*   *   *

The clean–up of your garden after harvest is actually an important step to the proper set–up of a garden for the next seed planting. Remember, one season feeds into another— it's like a circle.

Once your plants have given you food and are no longer productive, you will need to pull them out by the root and put them into your composter. If you are not composting, dispose of them into your waste bin. Plants left rotting in a container are a primary location source to harbor pests through inclement weather and usher them into a massive infestation come warm, sunny days.

Dispose of the container soil by dispersing it onto your grass or into other plant beds. If you happen to have fruit trees, the soil makes a great addition around their basins. A spade may be necessary to assist you in completing the task.

Some of the soil can be left in the container and used as a catalyst to make small portions of leaf humus. Position the container in the sunniest spot where it can stay while not in use. Then, simply layer damp soil and damp leaves, damp soil and damp leaves—until the container is full. Cover the container with a heavy plastic trash bag. In several months, just in time for your next planting, the leaves will have decomposed into the soil and provided for a rich, earthy beginning again.

*   *   *

Spring brings us the promise of renewal. The rising warmth of the sun bodes of promising beginnings.

Summer delivers on Spring's promise. It is a fulfillment.

Fall reminds us that, as with all things, there must be closure. We accept this.

Winter lets us rest and reflect.

*   *   *

Such is the cycle of the earth— and, of life.

Appendix I

OR

A Glossary of a Certain Sort

We felt very strongly about our Glossary having a simple and direct, matter-of-fact, folksy approach. However, we need to advise you that some of our 'definitions' are actual definitions, whereas others lean toward usage opinions. This section has a focus which is primarily task-based, in that it defines words within the manner for which we use them…and not always, or necessarily, as Webster may have done!

Should you require a more conventional word search for matters unrelated to the subject matter of this book, we urge you to pick up a standard dictionary.

Otherwise, we spell it out for you, in relation to the book, with our apologies to academia!

Aa

absorption: the uptake of substances, such as nutrients

activators: a catalyst

acuity: sharpness; acuteness; keenness

accommodations: adjustment of differences

adapt: -ed, -ing; adjust; modify; change to different conditions

adequate: as much or as good as necessary for some requirement or purpose; fully sufficient

adverse: in opposition; a contrary direction to what is favorable

advocate: one who is in strong favor of something; a person who speaks or writes supportively on behalf of a person or cause

aerate: -ed, -ing, -tion; to cause air circulation through or around something

allergen [environmental]: a natural [pollen, grasses, dust] or man–made [chemical or synthetic] substance that induces an allergy; the study of which is found under immunology

allergy [environmental]: a hypersensitive reaction of the body to allergen

analogy: similar or comparable in form and/or function

ancestors: a person from whom one is descended

animal by-products: a secondary or incidental product manufactured by an animal, such as manure

annual: living only one growing season

anxieties: tensions

aphids: tiny yellowish-green insects that suck the sap from the stems and leaves of plants

aroma: an odor; an agreeable fragrance

aromatherapy: the use of fragrances to affect or alter a mood or behavior

assimilation: the total process of plant nutrition, including photosynthesis and the absorption of raw materials

Bb

backfill: -ed, -ing; to refill a hole

bagged soil: a commercially prepared product geared towards certain types of plant needs and available at most retail nurseries

bark: the external covering of the woody stems and branches of trees, separate from the wood itself

bat guano: see guano

benefit: something that is intrinsically good

beneficial: advantageous; helpful

biodiversity: a combination of related or different life and plant forms, with each being complimentary to the others and instrumental in the formation of a healthy ecosystem

blood meal: dried blood of animals, used as fertilizer

bolt: -ing; to produce flowers or seeds prematurely

bone meal: animal bones ground to a coarse powder and used as fertilizer

botanical: something which relates to, is made from or contains a plant

botanist: a specialist in botany

botany: the science of plants

bulb [garlic]: consisting of many cloves, this is the entire unit of edible garlic as it comes out of the soil

bush [plant variety]: any variety which is able to grow upright, without the use of a trellis or cage [as opposed to a vining variety]

bypasses: avoids; obstructs; goes around

by-product: a secondary product resultant from another function, can be either intended or unintended

Cc

cage: a metal enclosure which fits over or around a vining variety, affixed into the soil by prongs or attached with ties; the purpose of which is to provide support for the vines and weight of growing vegetables

capsicum: a preparation of the pepper plant, used as a condiment; the "hot" property of a chile

cells: the basic structural units of all organisms

channel: a course into which something can be directed

chemicals [synthetic]: substances produced by a chemical process; substances used in a chemical process

choice: the right, power or opportunity to choose

clove [garlic]: the individual parts of a garlic bulb; used for replanting new garlic or used fresh for cooking

commercial: a characteristic of commerce

commitment: a promise

compaction [soil]: densely packed soil, without aeration

complex: complicated or involved; referring to many inter-related functions within a single unit

compilation: a gathering of things; to put together

compost: a commercially produced or homemade soil mix containing decaying and decomposing materials, which results in a rich organic fertilizer used to feed plants

composter: a homemade or retail unit used to produce garden compost

compost tea: a liquid by-product made by soaking compost in water overnight

confinement: an enclosure within fixed boundaries

consideration: careful thought

container [gardening]: anything waterproof with drainage holes in the bottom of it that contains or can contain a plant; must be of a size corresponding to the current stage of plant root and growth needs

containment: something capable of holding or having a capacity for same

control: to dominate or have command over someone or something

conventional: in general agreement to that which is commonly accepted

cotton cake: compressed cotton seed, wherein the oil has been extracted

cotton seed: the seed of the cotton plant

cottonseed meal: pulverized cotton cake

creativity: your ability to break out of and away from the traditional ways of doing things and replace same with new and different methodology

crops: the cultivated yield of plants from the ground; food plants in the process of growth

crop rotation: the intentionally successive planting of crops in a specified order, designed to leave the soil nutrient–rich for the next crop due to the systematic depletion and enrichment of the soil by the current crop

cultivate: -tion; using a [hand] cultivator to rough up the surface of soil in order to aerate the soil, destroy weeds and preclude soil compaction

cultivator [hand]: a multi-pronged, hand-held tool used to cultivate soil around plants

Dd

dairy: milk or any product of milk, including butter, cheese, cream; milk in any derivative or processed form

decompose: the rotting and decaying of organic material

depth: a downward measurement beginning at the soil surface

determinant: a determining factor

determinate: a plant with vines or tendrils that end in a flower or bud and do not further elongate

disclaimer: a statement that disclaims responsibility

dispersed: scattered

displaced: moved out of the usual place

disposable income: the extra money left over after you take care of the truly important things in your life

diverse: various

dose: a substance or quantity of something given in a measured application

douse: drench

drainage holes: small holes or slits through which water exits the bottom of a planting container

Ee

earth: soil and/or dirt; where you live

ecosystem: an ecological system of plants, animals and related life forms existing within an environment

education: the acquisition of knowledge

elements: a natural environment as opposed to a contrived environment; weather conditions; the material substances of the universe [earth, water, air and fire]

energy: the ability to maintain a vigorous activity level

energy force: a capability of potency within and without the universe

enhance: to raise to a higher level

environment: all the natural factors which surround a living organism

environmental: of or pertaining to the environment

environmentalist: a person who works to guard and protect natural resources, terrain, ecosystems, plants and animals from the resultant choice making of other humans

eons: a long, long time…

equi-distant: of equal distance

evolve [botanical]: -ing; development through evolution; an adaptive state of survival in response to changing environmental conditions

exposure: a point or location of an object in regard to both the amount of sunlight and elements of weather it will receive

Ff

factors: something contributing to a result

fava [bean]: Old World broad beans

fellowship: the relation of being a human to another human

fertilize: to enrich the soil of garden plants with nutrients

fertilizer [organic]: any substance or compound that contains plenteous nutrients for botanical uses; manure [cow, chicken, horse, rabbit]

fluids: liquid substances

flush [to soil]: a rush of water

folksy: informality [as sometimes in usage of speech]

foreign: not belonging where found

forest: land thickly covered with trees and bush

fresh: optimum nutritional content; not preserved

full-cycle: arriving back at the original place after going through all developments

full-growth: the maximum growth potential of a botanical species, including root spread, stalk height and diameter fill

functionally connected: a structure with an intended and united purpose

fundamental: essential

fungi [plural of fungus]; [botanical]: detrimental organisms [mold, mildew, rust] that live by absorbing the organic material in and on plants

fungicide: a substance or preparation used to destroy fungi

Gg

garden: surface or container soil, where flowers, vegetables, fruits, bushes and/or herbs are grown

gardening [vegetable]: the act of cultivating botanical species for harvest

garlic spray: a mixture of minced and ground–up fresh garlic and water used in a sprayer to dissuade pests from nibbling on your growing crops, leaves, stalks and the like

genealogy: -ical; the study and recordation of the ancestry or descent of a person, family or species

genes: the basic and tangible unit of lineage which includes DNA and when manifest, provides for the hereditary being and characterization of a species

genetic: anything related to, or produced by, genes

genetic engineering [botany]: the manipulation of genetic material to change the hereditary traits of a cell, organism or complete species

germinant: germinating

germinate: the beginning of growth or development

glands: a cell, group of cells or organ which produces a secretion and synergizes as a one dependent part to both other dependent parts and to the whole, for the routine life support of a species

goal: the result of directed or concentrated effort

go to seed: see bolting

gouge: to dig into and force an opening

green: not ripe

greens: green leafy vegetables

guano: a natural manure

Hh

hardy: -ier; sturdy; capable of surviving in extreme exposure or handling conditions

harvest: the collection of crops; the time when ripe crops are collected

health: the overall status of someone or something as regards it being free from disease and/or ailing condition

herbal: pertaining to herbs

herbs: a flowering plant used for medicinal purposes, cooking, or aromatherapy

herbicides: a substance or preparation to kill plant life

heirloom [seeds]: the possession of food plant seeds handed down from generation to generation

holism: -tic; a functional theory involving a system of naturopathic or chiropractic therapy, usually involving nutritional measures, outside the mainstream of scientific medicine

homeopathy: -ic; a methodology of treating infirmity or disease by a series of specific natural drugs or compounds

humus: the dark, organic material in soil which is produced by the decomposition of organic matter and is absolutely essential to the fertility of the earth

Ii

illness: sickness; poor health

immune system: a complex connection of cells and tissues that guards the body from pathogens and foreign substances, it destroys infected or malignant cells and funnels old cells out of the system

inability: lack of ability; incapability

infestation: an invasion

ingest: to take, as in food or supplement, into the body

inherent: a permanent genetic quality, characteristic or attribute of someone or something

inorganic: not living or having the metabolic structures of something that lived

irradiate: to treat something by exposure to radiation (as in or through the use of ultraviolet light)

insecticide: a substance or preparation used for killing insects

interdependency: mutually dependent; in dependence upon each other

interval: a period of time

Jj/Kk/Ll

Jack: an Alaskan malamute rescue dog of unknown lineage; lived to be nearly fifteen years of age; allowed toddler to learn to walk by holding his fur; loved the following in an ever-changing order until his last breath; his family, the outdoors, walks, other dogs, other people, morning biscuits and evening dinner

lace wing: small flying insects with delicate lace-like wings, the larvae of which preys on aphids

lady bug: small, round spotted beetle which feeds mainly on aphids

life: the condition or presence which distinguishes an organic being from an inorganic object via the manifestation of growth through an internal metabolism

life scientist: a person who studies living organism and their life processes

limbs: legs or arms

lodge: when vegetable crops fall over and lay flat, due to inclement weather such as rain, hail or high winds

Mm

maintenance: upkeep; support

manure: the excrement of animals [such as chickens, horses, rabbits or bats] used for fertilizer

matter-of-fact: factual; not subject to opinion

mature: something fully and completely developed in growth

mental: of the mind

metabolize: -ed; the process of organic functioning

methodology: a system or way of doing things

microwaves: -able; electromagnetic waves of extremely high frequency that when used in cooking, encapsulates and directs the waves to penetrate food, causing its molecules to vibrate and generate heat within the food, thus shortening the cooking time

mildew: a plant disease caused by fungi [looks like a wispy, cotton-like substance that is found on the surface of leaves or stalks]

mildewcide: a synthetic chemical used to destroy the disease of mildew

mitigate: lessen

moist: damp; slightly wet

moisten: to make moist

moisture: enough liquid to make or become moist

mulch: a covering of the soil underneath or around the base of plants, consisting of mature compost, straw or sheeting used to prevent weeds and assist the soil in retaining moisture

multitudinous: a large quantity; making a great number; very numerous

Nn

Nana: a Scottish grandmother who was orphaned at age 4, had a second grade education, lived to be 100 years and 1 month old, and who loved the following in an ever-changing order, [excepting the first one]; God, a hearty meal of fresh foods, the outdoors, coffee, animals, the desert, a hot cup of tea, peace and quiet, Guinness's Stout once-in-a-blue-moon, bright colors and me

nature: the world that exists independent of human beings or civilized input; elements of the natural world; the universe

natural: formed by nature; existing in a natural world as opposed to a man-made one

naturalize: to comfort to the standards of nature

negligent: to be without care

nervous system: in entirety, the functional connections of nerves and nerve controls in an animal or human, including the brain and spinal cord

nutrition: nourishment

nutritive: pertaining to nutrition

Oo

open-pollinated: a naturally occurring pollination process where-in a botanical species creates pollen and freely transfers it between itself and any other plant of the same botanical species via insects, birds or air current

opinion: a personal view

opportunistic: causing disease only under certain conditions

organ: connective tissues with a specialized task within the life form of a species

organic: pertaining to or obtained from living organisms

organisms: any life form considered self–contained

orientation: one's position in relation to an object, like the sun

Pp

pathogen: any disease producing substance; bacteria or virus

personal choice: your right, power or opportunity to choose

pesky: bothersome

pest defense: the pro-active nutritive balance of a plant which provides an environment adverse to pest infestation

pesticides: a chemical preparation used to destroy pests

pests: an insect or small animal that chews or distresses garden plants

planters: a container, in various shapes and sizes, used for growing plants

plenteous: high yielding; abundant; plentiful

pole [bean]: a vining variety of beans that must be trellised or staked

pollen: the fertilizing property of flowering plants which supplements pollination; appearance is that of powdery, yellowish, soft granules

pollinate: the movement of pollen from one stigma of a flower to another by insects, birds or air current

pollination: the completed action of pollen transfer, necessary for the cycle of fruition and resultant crop formation

positive: constructive and certain

posterity: that which we choose to leave behind for the intended benefit of those who follow our path

preclude: to prevent the occurrence of something happening

pre-destiny: decreed in advance

pre-packaged: goods [foodstuffs] which are packaged before distribution to retailers

preservatives: a chemical substance used to preserve foods from decomposing; utilized by manufacturers and distributors to elongate shelf-life of pre-packaged foods

preserve: -ed; to prepare and store food so that it does not decompose

primary: the first stage in any process

pro-active: taking initiative

processed: prepared or modified by an artificial method; foodstuffs which are derivative modifications of the initial food product

produce: the harvest of vegetables and fruits; perishables

productive: generative; producing abundantly

progress: forward or upward advancement towards a goal

prolific [harvest]: producing in large quantities

promise: assurance upon which a reasonable expectation may be placed

prongs: the pointed tines of an object

properties: attributes or qualities

proportion: the compared and contrasted spacial or relative dimension of an object to the physical environment in which it is placed

psychologist: a specialist in the science of the mind, mental states and processes

Qq

quality: character or nature of someone or something as regards fineness or excellence

quantity: an exact or specific amount of measure

Rr

rancid: rank or unpleasant smell or taste through decomposition

ready-made: pre–made for immediate use

recyclable: to make something adaptable for a new use without changing the original form

refrigerator pickles: home–made pickles

religion: a particular belief or following concerning creationism and morals

replenishable: to use again or anew

reproduce: to produce again or anew by natural process

researcher: investigator

residual: remaining; leftover

resignation: acquiescence; submission

resistance: the act or power of withstanding

retain: to hold or to have

reusable: something that can supply a usage beyond the initial intention

ritual: established or prescribed procedures

root ball: the roots and attached soil that is transplanted with a plant

roots: a downward growth of a plant into the soil which holds the plant within the soil and provides a route to absorb nutrients and moisture

rotation: see **crop rotation** and **sun rotation**

rudimentary: primitive

Ss

sage: wise

saturate: to soak thoroughly or completely

scquwoooogy: something that is sopping wet; the sound that an object which is full of water makes when you pick it up

secondary: next, as in an ordinal listing; of a lesser importance

seed bed: soil prepared for seedlings

seeds: a fertilized and matured ovule of a flowering plant which contains an embryo of the plant

seedling: a very young plant which has been grown from a seed

self-contained: containing in itself all that is necessary

shock: a sudden and intense disturbance

shoots: a side vine or like growth of a plant or tree

sickly: unhealthy

signature leaves: leaves which bear a true and independent resemblance to the botanical variety of a plant; leaves which provide a botanical identification of a species due to their significant shape, color and form

soap spray: a mixture of mild biodegradable liquid soap and water applied from a sprayer onto pests located under leaves or within the stalks or crevices of your plants

soggy: soaked; thoroughly wet and sodden

soil: humus rich ground or earth used for growing crops

spacial perspective: the physical relationship of one object to another object or group of objects within a contained environment in a manner visually pleasing to the eye; a direct and measured relationship of one part of an object to an interfacing part of another object

species: a biological or horticultural classification of a plant

spritz: to spray briefly and quickly; to squirt

sprout: to begin to grow and shoot forth, as in from a seed to a seedling to a plant

staking: support to a vining plant by the use of stakes driven into the soil surrounding the plant

stalk: the stem of a plant

stamina: physical strength and/or ability to endure disease or fatigue

stratify: lightly scratching the side or face of a seed to hasten or aid germination; layering seeds between soil to germinate

structured: a clearly defined organization

succumb: yield to disease

summer [variety]: annual food plants germinated or budding in late spring and harvested in early through late summer

sun rotation: the placement of a plant in accordance with the amount of direct or indirect sunlight which it may receive

sunshine: direct light of the sun

supporter: advocate

supportive: additional assistance

surrender: to give up something to the influence of another

synthetic: something produced by a chemical process

Tt

task-based: piece work that is goal–oriented

tendrils: runners; vines; long, thin growth extensions of a plant used for climbing and attaching to a trellis

theory: the principle points of an explanation

tissues: similar or like cells that form a structured material or presence and have a specific function

tools: an implement, usually hand–held, for doing work of a specific nature

topical: an external application

traditional (seeds): handed down by tradition

transplant: to remove a plant from one location and replant it in another

trellis: a framework of wood or wire, supplanted into the soil of a plant and used as a support for vining plants

trimming: pieces cut off in the trimming, clipping or pruning of trees, plants or the like

true leaves: the beginning and signature leaves of a plant after the seed pod has opened

true to form: the ability of consistent varietal reproduction as regards the genetic values, characteristics, propensities and traits that is inherent within seeds created in a naturally occurring phenomena and not a man–made sequence; the reproductive ability of a traditional or heirloom seed

truth: that which is genuine and actual

Uu

ultraviolet light: used in the irradiation of meats, fruits, vegetables, herbs...

umbrel: a flowering, then seed–producing umbrella shaped growth or extension of a plant

unstructured: without formal organization

usage opinion: a personal view of how to apply something

usages: applications

Vv

varietal: characteristic of a variety

variety: [**botanical**] different types of plants, although within the same general category or species

vigor: endurance; potency

vine: -ing; plants with long stems that creep on the ground or climb and hold onto supports with tendrils

vital: energetic; necessary to life

volunteer: a plant that grows without being seeded, planted or cultivated (usually by loose seeds that have fallen unawares), and germinates when the conditions are proper for that particular variety

Ww

waste: a cast off from a primary source

weakness: lack of vigor

weed: a worthless plant that pops up and if left, will rob the primary plant of nutrients and eventually suffocate the heck out of it

wholesome: contributing to health

worms: invertebrate life form which crawls on the ground or in sub–soil and may also climb [some worms are good, some worms are bad— around here though, "We brake for earthworms."]

Xx/Yy/Zz

A word or two about these letters...

While others scramble to seek to fill something, we simply choose to admit...this is it!

Appendix II

OR

Resources

As of this printing, all of the following companies and their products were available.

Seeds of Change
1.888.762.7333
www.seedsofchange.com
Heirloom and traditional seeds catalogue orders
(call to obtain a free catalogue, then
order by mail, phone, online or fax)

Harmony Catalog
360 Interlocken Blvd., Suite 300
Broomfield, CO 80021–3440
www.gaiam.com
1.800.869.3446
Gardening supplies
(call for a free catalogue)

Kellogg Supply, Inc.
Carson, CA. 90745
1.310.830.2200

(This company manufactures and distributes organic fertilizer, however it is via the wholesale market only. Ask your local nursery if they can order for you.)

Afterthoughts...

There is no way I could publish this without including some reflection upon the situations which occurred during the book's scripting. It would be unthinkable to do so. Sigh. The problem is, where to begin...and what I want to say and commit to posterity.

My grandmother died during the time I was writing this. She was the one who first showed me how *valuable* soil was. After she died, it was very hard to apply myself and write about the subject matter of gardening. I almost gave up on this book.

I lost a really neat friend during this time, though not in the same way as my grandmother. But, a loss is a loss.

My dog, a 15 year companion, was put down.

I suffered an injury which had me both on crutches and the disabled list for a few weeks. That was really a tough one. I am accustomed to being very physically active and the inability to be so was extremely difficult to work through.

We endured umpteen dozen familial struggles and thankfully, almost the same amount of successes— the jury is still out on a few.

There was a lot of darkness in my field of vision. Work, eat, sleep. Work, eat, sleep. Work, be too tired to eat, try to sleep.

While this isn't everything, I trust you get the picture.

I believed then, as I believe now, that some of us must simply have a genetic buoyancy for survival—a physical and mental survival—that allows us to keep pedaling...keep treading water...keep functioning and to effectively continue to manage our lives.

I also believe that, at times, some of us have a message, some of us are messengers, and that some of us are intended recipients. I adjudged that this book fit into that frame of reference somewhere. It was then that I started to see some color in an otherwise gray palette.

I hope that you always find the strength which you need to help you work through your difficulties. I hope that when darkness comes in your direction, it has a short stay. I wish for you the knowledge that there is a balance to our lives, and that sometimes one just has to rely on this belief when all facts appear to the contrary.

I wish you peace.

E.L.

About the Author

Eileen Logan is an elementary school teacher in the Los Angeles area. She has authored and illustrated a book of parables, as well as two children's stories. Eileen is currently working on a commissioned biography which includes genealogical research. She has recently expanded her writing into creative ventures, including novels and movie screenplays.

In spite of this busy schedule, Eileen remains an active participant in environmental and community issues.

Also by Eileen Logan:

"Humanity without Fear;
a surrender to the full spectrum of light"

—

Other works-in-progress by Eileen Logan:

"95 Slateford Road;
A biography of a certain nature"

the end

0-595-21772-9

Printed in the United Kingdom
by Lightning Source UK Ltd.
123258UK00002B/299/A